SHORT WALKS
EXMOOR

by Steve Davison

Walkers heading towards Great Rowbarrow (Walk 10)

CONTENTS

Using this guide 4
Route summary table 6
Map key 7
Introduction 9
  Walking on Exmoor 10
  Where to stay 11
  Travel 11

The walks

1. Combe Martin and Great Hangman 13
2. Hunter's Inn and Martinhoe 19
3. Lynton and the Valley of Rocks 23
4. Lynmouth and Watersmeet 29
5. The Foreland 35
6. Simonsbath and the Barle Valley 41
7. Lorna Doone Country 47
8. Porlock Weir and Culbone church 53
9. Tarr Steps and the River Barle 59
10. Dunkery Beacon 63
11. Allerford and Selworthy 69
12. Dulverton and Marsh Bridge 75
13. Haddon Hill and Wimbleball Lake 79
14. Luxborough and Withycombe Common 83
15. Dunster and Bat's Castle 89

Useful information 95

USING THIS GUIDE

Routes in this book

In this book you will find a selection of easy or moderate walks suitable for almost everyone, including casual walkers and families with children, or for when you only have a short time to fill. The routes have been carefully chosen to allow you to explore the area and its attractions. Most routes are circular or out-and-back, although some linear walks may be included that use public transport to get back to the start. Although there may be some climbs there is no challenging terrain, but do bear in mind that conditions can sometimes be wet or muddy underfoot. A route summary table is included on page 6 to help you choose the right walk.

Clothing and footwear

You won't need any special equipment to enjoy these walks. The weather in Britain can be changeable, so choose clothing suitable for the season and wear or carry a waterproof jacket. For footwear, comfortable walking boots or trainers with a good grip are best. A small rucksack for drinks, snacks and spare clothing is useful. See www.adventuresmart.uk.

Walk descriptions

At the beginning of each walk you'll find all the information you need:

- start/finish location, with postcode and a what3words address to help you find it
- parking and transport information, estimated walking time, total distance and climb
- details of public toilets available along the route and where you can get refreshments
- a summary of the key highlights of the walk and what you might see

Timings given are the time to complete the walk at a reasonable walking pace. Allow extra time for extended stops or if walking with children.

The route is described in clear, easy-to-follow directions, with each waypoint marked on an accompanying map extract. It's a good idea to read the whole of the route instructions before setting out, so that you know what to expect.

Maps, GPX files and what3words

Extracts from the OS® 1:25,000 map accompany each route. GPX files for all the walks in this book are available to download at www.cicerone.co.uk/1190/gpx.

What3words is a free smartphone app which identifies every 3m square of the globe with a unique three-word address, e.g. ///destiny.cafe.sonic. For more information see https://what3words.com/products/what3words-app.

USING THIS GUIDE

Walking with children

Even young children can be surprisingly strong walkers, but every family is different and you may need to adapt the timings given in this book to take that into account. Make sure you go at the pace of the slowest member and choose a walk with an exciting objective in mind, such as a cave, river, waterfall or picnic spot. Many of the walks can be shortened to suit – suggestions are included at the end of the route description.

Dogs

Sheep or cattle may be found grazing on a number of these walks. Keep dogs under control at all times so that they don't scare or disturb livestock or wildlife. Cattle, particularly cows with calves, may very occasionally pose a risk to walkers with dogs. If you ever feel threatened by cattle, you should let go of your dog's lead and let it run free.

Enjoying the countryside responsibly

Enjoy the countryside and treat it with respect to protect our natural environments. Stick to footpaths and take your litter home with you. When driving, slow down on rural roads and park considerately, or better still use public transport. For more details check out www.gov.uk/countryside-code.

The Countryside Code

Respect everyone
- be considerate to those living in, working in and enjoying the countryside
- leave gates and property as you find them
- do not block access to gateways or driveways when parking
- be nice, say hello, share the space
- follow local signs and keep to marked paths unless wider access is available

Protect the environment
- take your litter home – leave no trace of your visit
- do not light fires and only have BBQs where signs say you can
- always keep dogs under control and in sight
- dog poo – bag it and bin it – any public waste bin will do
- care for nature – do not cause damage or disturbance

Enjoy the outdoors
- check your route and local conditions
- plan your adventure – know what to expect and what you can do
- enjoy your visit, have fun, make a memory

ROUTE SUMMARY TABLE

WALK NAME	START POINT	TIME	DISTANCE
1. Combe Martin and Great Hangman	Combe Martin	2¾hr	8km (5 miles)
2. Hunter's Inn and Martinhoe	Heddon Valley	2¼hr	7km (4¼ miles)
3. Lynton and the Valley of Rocks	Lynton	3hr	8.5km (5¼ miles)
4. Lynmouth and Watersmeet	Hillsford Bridge	3hr	8km (5 miles)
5. The Foreland	Barna Barrow	2½hr	7km (4¼ miles)
6. Simonsbath and the Barle Valley	Simonsbath	3½hr	11km (6¾ miles)
7. Lorna Doone Country	County Gate	2hr	6.5km (4 miles)
8. Porlock Weir and Culbone church	Porlock Weir	3hr	8.5km (5¼ miles)
9. Tarr Steps and the River Barle	Tarr Steps	1½hr	4.5km (2¾ miles)
10. Dunkery Beacon	Dunkery Gate and Bridge	2¾hr	7.5km (4¾ miles)
11. Allerford and Selworthy	Allerford	2¾hr	8.5km (5¼ miles)
12. Dulverton and Marsh Bridge	Dulverton	2hr	5.5km (3½ miles)
13. Haddon Hill and Wimbleball Lake	Haddon Hill	2½hr	8km (5 miles)
14. Luxborough and Withycombe Common	Luxborough	2¾hr	9km (5½ miles)
15. Dunster and Bat's Castle	Dunster	2¼hr	7km (4½ miles)

ROUTE SUMMARY TABLE

HIGHLIGHTS
Village, clifftop walk, coastal views
Coastal views, oak woods, historic carriageway
Cliff railway, coast path, rock formations
Wooded valley, riverside, historic tea room
Coast path, woods, views, Countisbury hamlet
Two Moors Way, River Barle, Iron Age hill fort
Doone Valley, two rivers and rural hamlets
Pretty harbour village, woods
Ancient clapper bridge, woods, River Barle
Exmoor's highest summit, views, open moor
Picturesque hamlets, coastal views
Historic market town, riverside paths, woods
Views, Exmoor ponies, open heathland
Three peaceful hamlets, views, woods
Historic town, Iron Age hill fort, views

SYMBOLS USED ON ROUTE MAPS

S   Start point

F   Finish point

SF   Start and finish at the same place

    Waypoint

～   Route line

MAPPING IS SHOWN AT A SCALE OF 1:25,000

```
0 KM      0.25       0.5
|----|----|----|----|
0 miles        0.25
```

DOWNLOAD THE GPX FILES FOR FREE AT
www.cicerone.co.uk/1190/gpx

Following the Two Moors Way alongside the River Barle (Walk 6)

INTRODUCTION

Exmoor pony grazing on Gallox Hill, with Dunkery Beacon behind to the left (Walk 15)

Exmoor, a national park since 1954, covers an area of 692km² (267 square miles) straddling the border between Somerset and Devon in south-west England. Once a royal hunting forest, Exmoor offers a varied landscape of moorland, ancient woodland, tree-shaded river valleys and coastal cliffs where the land drops steeply into the Bristol Channel.

Shaped by humans over thousands of years (there are several Bronze Age barrows on the high moor), Exmoor is a working, agricultural landscape of open heathland and small fields separated by high hedgerows formed of earth banks, faced with stone or turf and topped with shrubs. Hidden amongst the rolling hills and valleys are small towns and villages offering cosy pubs and historic buildings. But there is also a diverse wildlife, from Exmoor ponies to the largest number of wild red deer in England.

Many artists and writers, including poets such as Coleridge and Wordsworth, have taken inspiration from Exmoor's landscape. Head to the Badgworthy Water and you can walk through the pages of *Lorna Doone*, R D Blackmore's tale of love and derring-do set in 17th-century Exmoor.

As well as offering some lovely walking opportunities – from the windswept expanse of Dunkery Beacon (Exmoor's highest hill at 519m) to the fascinating rock structures of the Valley of Rocks – Exmoor is a great place to gaze at the heavens, a fact confirmed when the national park was designated as Europe's first International Dark Sky Reserve in 2011.

Walking on Exmoor

The walks in this guidebook are designed to show the varied nature of Exmoor, from high moors to tranquil woodland and from gentle riverside paths to hilly coastal paths; five of the walks explore sections of the South West Coast Path, offering lovely coastal views.

The routes are generally well signposted and follow fairly well-used paths. They can be enjoyed all year round; however, some of the paths may be wet and rather muddy, especially during the winter months and some of the walks have streams to cross with no footbridges. In spring there is an abundance of flowers and new growth, summer brings the largest number of visitors, while in autumn the woodlands put on a colourful display and a crisp, frosty winter's day can be magical. The temperature and weather can change quickly on the open moor, so it is always a good idea to carry some extra clothing just in case.

The walks, which are all circular, explore many interesting places across Exmoor, including the fascinating Valley of Rocks (Walk 3), the ancient Tarr Steps clapper bridge (Walk 9), the

Heading towards Silcombe Farm (Walk 8)

Looking to Castle Rock in the Valley of Rocks (Walk 3)

lofty heights of Dunkery Beacon (Walk 10) and historic Dulverton (Walk 12). There is also a more challenging route (Walk 6) that explores the peaceful River Barle valley near Simonsbath.

While you are out walking, make time to soak in the views, look for wildlife, enjoy a picnic, or explore the historic towns and villages. You could visit Dunster Castle, a local museum, or take a ride on the world-famous Lynton and Lynmouth Cliff Railway. But most of all, enjoy and respect the unique landscape, wildlife and character of Exmoor.

Where to stay

Exmoor offers a wide range of accommodation, from campsites and youth hostels to pubs with rooms and hotels. There are several towns and larger villages, such as Combe Martin, Dunster, Dulverton, Lynmouth and Lynton, and Porlock, that offer accommodation and other services, including transport links, restaurants, pub, cafes and shops. Some smaller villages offer a pub with rooms or a guesthouse. Outside the national park larger towns include Barnstaple, Ilfracombe, Minehead, Tiverton, and Watchet.

Travel

The most useful stations for reaching Exmoor are Barnstaple, with rail connections to Exeter, and Taunton, with rail connections to the South-West, London, the Midlands and the North.

The harbour at Porlock Weir (Walk 8)

There are no train stations within Exmoor National Park.

Several of the walks start at or near public transport links, as detailed in the walk information. Useful bus services include the Exmoor Coaster bus, which operates between Minehead and Lynmouth (excluding winter), while Barnstaple has bus links to Lynmouth and Combe Martin, and Taunton has bus links to Dulverton. There are also more local bus services, but it is worth noting that these services may be quite infrequent.

If travelling by car, the M5, which links the Midlands to the South-West, passes to the south of Exmoor; the M4, which links London and Wales, connects with the M5 at Bristol. Several main A-roads travel north into Exmoor, from where a network of narrow roads and lanes spread out, some of these being narrow lanes with passing places. When driving through Exmoor, keep a lookout for animals and livestock, especially on unfenced roads, and always park in the car parks provided.

WALK 1
Combe Martin and Great Hangman

Start/finish	Combe Martin Museum, Cross Street
Locate	///beginning.respect.curvy
Cafes/pubs	Pubs and cafes in Combe Martin
Transport	Bus links to Ilfracombe and Barnstaple
Parking	Kiln car park on Cross Street, off A399 in Combe Martin (EX34 0DH)
Toilets	At car park

Combe Martin, tucked on the western edge of Exmoor, is the start point for a coastal walk along part of the South West Coast Path high above sea cliffs, visiting Little and Great Hangman for some brilliant views. Back in the village visit the museum or head to the beach. A shorter walk to Little Hangman is also possible.

Time 2¾hr
Distance 8km (5 miles)
Climb 390m

A hilly coastal walk from Combe Martin, offering views from Little and Great Hangman

The beach at Combe Martin

1 Facing the **museum** in Cross Street, turn left to a junction and turn right. Head up through the car park to a junction and bear right up the lane, passing the national park sign. After 25m turn left following the signed coast path up along the top edge of Cobbler's Park above the upper car park, keeping the wall on your right. Then continue steeply up to a junction above **Lester Cliff** and bear left (signed to Great Hangman). Keep ahead at the next path junction and follow the coast path through the small gate. Continue to another junction and fork left. The right-hand fork leads to West Challacombe for the shorter walk.

2 Continue up the coast path and near the top of the rise fork left to the top of **Little Hangman**, with views to Combe Martin Bay to the west and Great Hangman to the east. Return to the coast path and continue with a

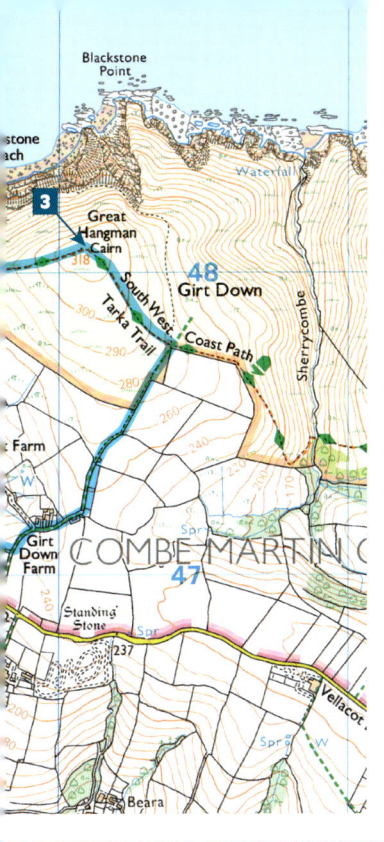

wall on your right and coast on your left. Keep ahead through two small gates and continue up to the stone cairn on the summit of **Great Hangman**. This is the highest point on the South West Coast Path and is also England's highest sea cliff at 244m.

3 Turn right, following the coast path down to a junction at the corner of a wall. Turn right (signed 'County Road'), leaving the coast path. Follow the wall on your left, go through a gate and continue across the field. Go through a gate and down the track, passing **Girt Down Farm**. Keep left at a junction up a short rise and turn right along the enclosed path (signed to Combe Martin), down to a minor road. Bear right down this for 70m, then turn right onto a track. The next section can be muddy; to miss this out continue down the road to a left-hand

Following the coast path up towards Little Hangman

Looking to Great Hangman from Little Hangman, with a clear view of the coast path

bend, keep ahead down the bridleway and cross a tarmac track to rejoin the walk from Waypoint 5.

4 Walk down the track and immediately after crossing a stream turn left. Go through a gate and follow the path down beside the tree-shaded stream. Go through another gate and continue along the track to a junction (the shortcut via West Challacombe joins from the right). Continue along the tarred track to a junction and take the second path on the right (signed to the beach).

5 Follow the enclosed path down to a lane and bear left, passing a school. On reaching the A399 road, turn right. Along the road to the left is the Pack o' Cards Inn (600m each way). Having turned right, after 50m, fork right along Cross Street back to the museum on your right. To visit the beach keep ahead to the junction and follow Cross Street to the left and then turn right.

WALK 1 – COMBE MARTIN AND GREAT HANGMAN

On the way to Great Hangman looking back to Little Hangman

▬ To shorten

From Little Hangman retrace your steps to Waypoint 2 and turn left. Go through a gate and head down to West Challacombe, then continue towards Combe Martin and rejoin the main walk at a junction with a tarred track just before Waypoint 5. This shortens the walk by 4.5km (1hr 15min) and saves 140m of climb.

Combe Martin

The linear village of Combe Martin stretches along a narrow valley for 2.5km, ending at a small beach. It is in the Guinness Book of Records for holding the longest street party. Along the main street is the unusual 17th-century Pack o' Cards Inn, built to resemble a 'house of cards', and the 13th-century Church of St Peter ad Vincula. Visit the local history museum in Cross Street to learn more about Combe Martin.

Seat on The Carriageway looking to the Valley of Rocks and The Foreland

WALK 2
Hunter's Inn and Martinhoe

Time 2¼hr
Distance 7km (4¼ miles)
Climb 310m

Coastal views, a historic carriageway, oak woods and a bit of Roman history

Start/finish	Hunter's Inn, Heddon Valley
Locate	///period.reworked.rides
Cafes/pubs	Pub and cafe at Heddon Valley
Transport	No public transport
Parking	Heddon Valley National Trust car park, signposted off A39 (EX31 4PY)
Toilets	At car park

From the Hunter's Inn, nestled in the steep-sided Heddon Valley, the walk makes a gradual ascent along a 19th-century carriageway with some lovely coastal views, passing oak woodland – keep a lookout for peregrine falcons and buzzards – and the site of a Roman fort. The return route takes you inland, passing through Martinhoe, before heading back along rather steep lanes and through fields down to the valley.

The Hunter's Inn, Heddon Valley

SHORT WALKS EXMOOR

1 From the National Trust car park turn left along the road, passing the National Trust cafe on your right, to a junction in front of the **Hunter's Inn**. Turn right for a few paces, then fork left along the track (bridleway) with the inn on your left. At the Y-junction fork right, signed to Woody Bay. The left-hand fork leads to Heddon's Mouth for a longer walk. Continue along the track, known as 'The Carriageway', up through **Road Wood**. After leaving the trees the route makes a big loop as it crosses Hill Brook and continues up to reach the coast above **Highveer Rocks** with views across the Bristol Channel to Wales and along the coast.

WALK 2 – HUNTER'S INN AND MARTINHOE

2 Follow the track to the right, keeping parallel to the coastline, with views ahead to the Valley of Rocks and The Foreland. On the way, a signed path on the right leads up to The Beacon, the site of a Roman fortlet. The track meanders its way through areas of sessile oak and whitebeam and crosses the **Hollow Brook**. Go through a gate and continue through **West Woodybay Wood** and keep ahead to reach a lane at a bend.

3 Turn sharp right (almost doubling back) and follow the path slightly uphill. Go left at a path junction to join a lane. Turn right and follow the lane to **Martinhoe**, taking care at the blind corner. Martinhoe is home to the Old Rectory Hotel and St Martin's Church which dates from the late 13th and early 14th century. Continue along the lane for 500m, soon heading gently downhill and turn right off the road at a fingerpost, signed to Hunter's Inn.

4 Go through the field gate and continue along the right-hand field edge to the corner. Turn left downhill and then turn right through a gate. Continue down the wooded path beside a stream on your left. Keep ahead through two gates, then bear left along the track past **Mannacott**

St Martin's Church at Martinhoe

Following the bridleway back down to the valley

Farm. Join **King's Lane** at a hairpin bend and turn right, heading steeply downhill. After passing the access road for Heddon's Gate Hotel on the right, continue for a further 150m, then fork left along a bridleway. Follow this down through the trees to a lane and turn sharp right back to the car park.

> ### ✚ To lengthen
> At the Y-junction, after passing the Hunter's Inn, fork left and follow the waymarked route (bridleway to Heddon's Mouth) alongside the River Heddon, later crossing the river via the footbridge to visit Heddon's Mouth, a rocky cove with a stone-and-shingle beach and old lime kiln at the mouth of the River Heddon. Then retrace your steps. This adds 1.5km (30min).

> ### Martinhoe and the Hunter's Inn
> In 1885 'Colonel' Benjamin Lake bought the Martinhoe Manor estate, with grand plans to make Woody Bay into a tourist destination. By 1899 he had built a pier in Woody Bay so that steamers carrying wealthy travellers could dock, allowing passengers to be transported by horse and carriage along 'The Carriageway' to the Hunter's Inn; the walk follows part of this carriageway. However, Lake was soon declared bankrupt and his grand plans were never realised.

WALK 3
Lynton and the Valley of Rocks

Start/finish	*Bottom Meadow car park, Lynton*
Locate	*///cadet.sharpened.added*
Cafes/pubs	*Pubs and cafes in Lynton, tea room at Valley of Rocks (200m off route)*
Transport	*Buses from Barnstaple to Lynmouth stop at the car park in Lynton*
Parking	*Bottom Meadow car park along Castle Hill in Lynton (EX35 6JD)*
Toilets	*At start and at Valley of Rocks (200m off route)*

Time 3hr
Distance 8.5km (5¼ miles)
Climb 410m

A coastal walk exploring the fascinating Valley of Rocks and climbing South Cleave and Hollerday Hill

From Lynton this rollercoaster walk follows the coast path past the fascinating Valley of Rocks. On reaching Lee Abbey it's a stiff climb before following the other side of the valley for more views. After dropping back into the valley the last section skirts round Hollerday Hill then heads back to Lynton. A shorter walk misses out the hilly bit above Lee Abbey. While you are in Lynton take a ride on the world-famous cliff railway.

Looking back along the Valley of Rocks to Hollerday Hill

1 Exit the car park and turn left up Castle Hill to a junction, immediately after passing St Mary's Church on your right. Turn right down North Walk Hill, following the footpath to Lynmouth and Valley of Rocks. As the road levels out the coast path joins from the right (having come up from Lynmouth). Continue along the lane (North Walk) to cross a bridge over the **cliff railway**.

2 Keep straight ahead, following the coast path. Go through a gate, leaving the trees behind and continue as the path heads past rocky outcrops with the sea on your right. At the Y-junction, fork right along the coast path, passing below the **Rugged Jack** rock outcrop to a junction with seats, with Castle Rock ahead in the **Valley of Rocks**.

This fascinating dry valley runs parallel to the coast, with dramatic rock formations and beautiful scenery. It is home to feral goats that forage on the steep, rocky slopes.

3 Head over to the lane and turn right. Turn left for the shortcut along the lane past the tea garden. Follow the lane (or coast path) for 900m to reach the entrance tower of 19th-century **Lee Abbey** on your right.

Entrance tower at Lee Abbey

The Valley of Rocks is home to feral goats

View over the Valley of Rocks from Hollerday Hill

> ⓘ *Opposite Castle Rock on the other side of the valley is a rocky outcrop known as the Devil's Cheese Ring, reputedly home to a white witch known as Mother Meldrum who was mentioned by RD Blackmore in his novel Lorna Doone.*

4 Turn left along the track (signed to Six Acre Cross) to a track junction in **Six Acre Wood** and turn sharp left up to the next corner. Fork left (straight on) along the path (signed Lynton via Southcliffe) and go through a kissing gate. Follow the narrow path as it zigzags uphill, then follow the top of **South Cleave** before starting to descend with a wall

on your right, enjoying the views across the Valley of Rocks on the way. Come to a kissing gate.

5 Go through the gate and continue down to a junction. Turn left, with a wall on your right, and keep ahead down to a lane. Some 200m to the left is Mother Meldrum's tea garden. Turn right along the lane to a path junction on the left just before a cattle grid.

6 Turn left and immediately fork right (signed to Lynton via Hollerday Hill) following a zigzag path up to a junction. Turn right (signed to Lynton) skirting round **Hollerday Hill**. Go through a gate and continue down the track, still following signs for Lynton and ignoring side routes. On reaching Lee Road beside the town hall, turn left, soon passing the entrance to the Lynton and Lynmouth Railway on your left. Continue past St Mary's Church and retrace your steps to the car park.

– To shorten

At Waypoint 3 turn left along the lane, passing a car park with toilets and Mother Meldrum's Tea Garden on the left and then a car park on the right. Reach a path junction just before a cattle grid and rejoin the main route at Waypoint 6. This saves 4km (1hr 30min) and 210m of climbing.

Lynton and Lynmouth Cliff Railway

Lynton and Lynmouth Cliff Railway

The funicular railway joining the picturesque villages of Lynton and Lynmouth opened in 1890 and is the highest and steepest water-powered cliff railway in the world. It is also one of only three such railways that is fully water-powered and does not require water to be pumped back up to the top station (www.cliffrailwaylynton.co.uk). Take a ride down to bustling Lynmouth with its small tidal harbour overlooked by the Rhenish Tower on the pier (originally built as a navigation beacon and later used to store seawater for bathing).

WALK 4
Lynmouth and Watersmeet

Start/finish	*Hillsford Bridge (A39) near Lynmouth*
Locate	*///waters.optimists.look*
Cafes/pubs	*Tea room at Watersmeet, pubs and cafes in Lynmouth*
Transport	*Buses between Barnstaple and Minehead stop at Lynmouth (Waypoint 4)*
Parking	*Combe Park National Trust car park at Hillsford Bridge on A39 (EX35 6LE)*
Toilets	*In Lynmouth and at Watersmeet House*

Time 3hr
Distance 8km (5 miles)
Climb 440m

Follow the top of a wooded valley before descending to Lynmouth and returning along riverside and woodland paths

From Combe Park this walk follows the Two Moors Way, staying high above the valley and offering some good views. After dropping steeply down to Lynmouth and crossing the East Lyn River the route makes a more gradual climb up along the wooded East Lyn Valley to picturesque Watersmeet House. From here it's an easy walk following the Hoaroak Water back to the start.

Lynmouth harbour

1 Exit the car park, bear left to a T-junction beside **Hillsford Bridge** and turn left to the A39. Cross over with care and bear left, following the road up to the hairpin bend. Turn right (almost straight on) and up along the tree-shaded bridleway (signed 'Lynmouth and Two Moors Way'), passing the Iron Age earthworks of Myrtleberry South Enclosure, to reach a Y-junction.

2 Fork left and follow the **Two Moors Way** as it swings left to another signed junction. Take the right-hand fork (footpath to Lynton and Lynmouth) along the top of **Myrtleberry Cleave** and keep ahead, ignoring a path off to the right. Follow the narrow path as it zigzags down to cross a stream and then zigzags back uphill to a signed junction.

WALK 4 – LYNMOUTH AND WATERSMEET

3 Fork right (signed 'Lynmouth and Two Moors Way'), passing above **Oxen Tor**. At the split keep right, following the path towards Lynmouth, down through Lyn Cleave, later following the tarred path down between houses to the A39 in **Lynmouth**, opposite St John's Church.

4 Turn left, then right across the A39 (Watersmeet Road) and enter Lyndale car park (toilets). If you arrived by public transport, you will start the walk here. Head over to the riverside path and turn right (upstream), with the **East Lyn River** on your left. Ignore the first footbridge and then turn left at the next footbridge, crossing the river.

5 Once across the bridge turn right. Immediately the path splits – keep to the right-hand fork (signed to Watersmeet). Continue through **Wester Wood** with the river on your right to a Y-junction, signed 'Watersmeet Woodland Walk' and 'Watersmeet Riverside Walk'. Take the left-hand 'Woodland Walk' option up through the trees. Keep right at the split then left at the next junction, staying on the woodland route (right leads down to the river). At the next signed junction keep right in the direction of Watersmeet through **Horner's Neck Wood**. When you reach a stone bridge (on your right), keep ahead along the track with the river to your right, to **Watersmeet House**.

> Watersmeet House, a former fishing lodge built in 1832, sits at the confluence of the East Lyn River and the Hoaroak Water. It has been serving cream teas for over 120 years.

6 At Watersmeet House turn right across the footbridge over the **East Lyn**

The East Lyn River

Following the Two Moors Way after leaving Hillsford Bridge

Watersmeet House

River and turn right again. Just before the next footbridge, turn left up the steps (signed for Hillsford Bridge) and then turn right along a bridleway. Follow this up along the valley, keeping the Hoaroak Water on your right, to reach the B3223 road at **Hillsford Bridge**. Cross the road, turn right across the bridge, immediately turn left and then fork right back to the car park.

− To shorten

For a much shorter and flatter walk, at Waypoint 2 fork right down the path for Watersmeet. Cross the A39 and take the path opposite down to a junction, turn sharp left downstream then turn right across a stone bridge. Turn right again to Watersmeet House. Rejoin the main walk from Waypoint 6. This saves 4.5km (1hr 30min) and 300m of climbing.

Lynmouth

Picturesque Lynmouth is joined to its neighbour Lynton by a world-famous cliff railway (see Walk 3). The small tidal harbour looks out over Lynmouth Bay backed by Foreland Point and the wide expanse of the Bristol Channel. Less happily it is also known for the Lynmouth Flood. On the night of 15 August 1952, heavy rain over Exmoor turned the East Lyn River into a raging torrent that tore through Lynmouth. Sadly 34 people died and over 100 buildings were damaged or destroyed. Visit the National Park Centre along The Esplanade to learn more about Exmoor.

View to Lynton from the coast path at Butter Hill

WALK 5
The Foreland

Time 2½hr
Distance 7km (4¼ miles)
Climb 340m

A walk with some ups and downs, offering lovely coastal views and peaceful woodland

Start/finish	Barna Barrow, near Countisbury
Locate	///buzzing.strikers.dusty
Cafes/pubs	Pub at Countisbury (250m off route), honesty cafe at Gurney's Wood
Transport	Exmoor Coaster buses between Lynmouth (Ilfracombe) and Minehead stop at the Blue Ball Inn on the A39 (250m off route) – summer only
Parking	Barna Barrow car park on A39 (EX35 6NE)
Toilets	No public toilets on route

From Barna Barrow this route skirts round Butter Hill, high above the Bristol Channel, before heading down across The Foreland, Devon's most northerly point. The walk then meanders through peaceful woods before a stiff climb up to the open fields of Countisbury Common for an easier walk back to Barna Barrow. Just off the walk is the hamlet of Countisbury, with the historic Blue Ball Inn, which dates from the 13th century.

The Blue Ball Inn at Countisbury

SHORT WALKS EXMOOR

1 Head to the top of the car park and continue to reach a signed junction. Turn left and then keep left, following the wall on your left for 500m to a junction with the coast path, where the wall turns left – ahead is a seat with a view over to Lynton and Lynmouth.

To visit Countisbury turn left here, then bear right and left past a house and the church (right) and follow the tarmac track down to the A39 and the Blue Ball Inn (250m each way). If you arrived by public transport you will start the walk here.

2 Turn right, following the level coast path, skirting round the left side of **Butter Hill**. The path is narrow so take care. At the junction beside Great Red – a deep cleft seen on the left – continue down the coast path, following it as it curves right (do not fork left, as this takes you on a path that is

Heading through the wooded Glenthorne Cliffs

narrow and very exposed above a steep cliff). Continue downhill across **The Foreland**, later going down steps to a tarmac track in **Coddow Combe**. To visit the lighthouse on Foreland Point turn left. For the main route turn right up to the sharp right-hand bend.

Devon's most northerly point, The Foreland offers views along the Exmoor coastline and out over the Bristol Channel to Wales. The north-facing Foreland Lighthouse, which is still operational, was built in 1900 to aid shipping in the Bristol Channel.

3 On reaching the sharp bend fork left along the track (coast path). The shorter walk continues up the tarmac track. Immediately after passing a gate and stile (where there is an honesty cafe), turn right and follow the narrow coast path, passing a National Trust sign for Glenthorne Cliffs. Follow the undulating path through **Gurney's Wood** for 2km to a signed junction.

4 Turn sharp right (signed to Countisbury), following the path uphill

> ⓘ Exmoor has the longest stretch of broadleaved coastal woods in Britain, stretching from Countisbury to Porlock.

On the way back near Desolate Farm, looking to The Foreland

with great views. Immediately after passing a slight gully, turn left up to a junction with the access track from **Desolate Farm** on your left. Turn right along this and go through a gate to a path junction. Turn right across the field, go through a gate and continue across two more fields, aiming for the mast on Butter Hill. Continue over open ground, passing to the left of the trees and buildings at **Kipscombe Farm**. Cross straight over the tarmac access track and continue, keeping the boundary on your right, to a junction with another tarmac track. The shorter walk joins from the right here.

5 Cross straight over and follow the track signed to Lynmouth. Keep left at the split, then left at the next split to arrive at a junction passed earlier and turn left back to the car park.

> ⓘ *England's longest national trail, the South West Coast Path, stretches for 1015km from Minehead (Somerset) to South Haven Point (Dorset). It was originally used by coastguards on the lookout for smugglers.*

− To shorten

At Waypoint 3 continue up the tarmac track to the track junction at Waypoint 5 and turn right, rejoining the main walk. This shortens the walk by 2.5km (1hr) and saves 140m of climbing.

+ To lengthen

On joining the tarmac track in Coddow Combe turn left and follow the track down towards the lighthouse (private). Retrace your steps and continue uphill to Waypoint 3. This adds 1.5km (30min) to the walk.

The small footbridge on the way to Cow Castle

WALK 6
Simonsbath and the Barle Valley

Time 3½hr
Distance 11km (6¾ miles)
Climb 300m

A long walk in the Barle valley, following part of the Two Moors Way and visiting an Iron Age hill fort

Start/finish	Simonsbath
Locate	///home.recliner.whispers
Cafes/pubs	Pub and tea room (150m off route) at Simonsbath
Transport	No public transport
Parking	Ashcombe car park, Simonsbath (TA24 7SH)
Toilets	At car park

This is a fairly long walk, with most of the ups and downs in the first half, passing through farmland and returning along a remote valley. From Simonsbath the walk meanders up through Birchcleave Wood and then on through fields above the valley, before heading down to the River Barle. The return route follows the river and the Two Moors Way back to Simonsbath, passing the Iron Age earthworks of Cow Castle and the scant ruins of the Wheal Eliza copper mine.

Following the River Barle towards Birchcleave Wood

1 From the car park head back to the road (B3223) and turn right down past the Exmoor Inn to the right-hand bend. Turn left across the road to a track and fork left along the bridleway signed to Picked Stones. Within a few paces, at a three-way junction, take the middle bridleway (signed to Picked Stones) up through Birchcleave Wood. This is said to be the highest beech wood in England. Bear right along a track, soon curving left along the top edge of the wood. At the bridleway fingerpost turn right (signed to Picked Stones) through a gate.

2 Follow the left-hand field edge, go through two gates and continue across the next field with the boundary on your right. On reaching two gates go through the one on the left and follow the left-hand field edge through two fields. Keep ahead into a third field, passing **Winstitchen Farm** over to the left. Continue along the left-hand edge for 300m before turning left through a gate opening. Follow the left-hand edge through two more fields. In the third field keep ahead and after passing some trees, turn left through a gate. Now follow the track as it turns right downhill to a bridge.

3 Cross the bridge over the **White Water** and go through two gates. This valley was the site of the 19th-century Picked Stones Iron Mine.

43

View of Cow Castle after crossing the White Water at Picked Stones

Continue up the track and soon there is a good view of Cow Castle to the right. Go through a gate, follow the left-hand field edge and turn left through a gate. Follow the enclosed track, then bear right along the tarred track heading away from **Pickedstones Farm**. After passing the hedge, fork right through a gate along the bridleway signed to Withypool. Continue through the field and go through a gate on the far side to a cross-junction.

4 Turn right downhill for 750m to another junction and turn right again. The walk now follows the **Two Moors Way** back to Simonsbath. Go through the gate and keep ahead, passing through another gate to reach a junction. Keep ahead (ignoring the footbridge on the left over the river) and cross a small footbridge over the White Water, then go through a kissing gate. Keep left of a small knoll and then skirt round the right-hand side of **Cow Castle** before bearing left alongside a wall on your right. On approaching the River Barle, turn right to a gate.

> Crowning the prominent knoll are the earthworks of Cow Castle. This fairly small hill fort dates from the early Iron Age and consists of a single ditch and rampart. From the top of the defensive position there are good views along the valley.

5 Go through the gate and keep ahead with the river on your left for just over 1km, passing through gates to

arrive at the ruins of **Wheal Eliza**. Continue, passing to the right of a knoll (**Flexbarrow**) before following the river again upstream, going through two gates. At a Y-junction, fork right to take the bridleway to Simonsbath, then go through a gate and continue through Birchcleave Wood to another junction. Fork left to the road (B3223). To the left is the restored sawmill, Simonsbath House (now a hotel) and Boeveys Tea Room (150m each way). To finish the walk, cross the road and turn right up past the Exmoor Forest Inn and shortly turn left back to the car park.

Royal Forest of Exmoor and Simonsbath

Simonsbath House (now a hotel) was built in 1654 for James Boevey, warden of the Royal Forest of Exmoor, a royal hunting ground. For around 150 years, it was the only house within the forest boundary. The 'forest' was bought by John Knight in the early 19th century and he set about turning it into a more agriculture-based area, building a number of farms, including Pickedstones. He also built St Luke's Church (200m further up the B3223 from the car park entrance), planted Birchcleave Wood and built the water-powered sawmill opposite Simonsbath House.

Footbridge over the Badgworthy Water on the way to Clouds Farm

WALK 7
Lorna Doone Country

Start/finish	*County Gate*
Locate	*///direction.accusing.cactus*
Cafes/pubs	*Cafe at County Gate and in Malmsmead*
Transport	*Buses between Lynmouth and Minehead stop at County Gate on the A39*
Parking	*County Gate car park on A39 (EX35 6NY)*
Toilets	*At car park and in Malmsmead*

Time 2hr
Distance 6.5km (4 miles)
Climb 235m

Head to County Gate for a walk through Lorna Doone Country, visiting the villages of Malmsmead and Oare

From County Gate – at the junction of Devon and Somerset – the walk heads steeply down to the hamlet of Malmsmead with its picturesque 17th-century bridge and ancient ford. The route then follows the Badgworthy Water in the footsteps of the fictional Doone family from R D Blackmore's novel *Lorna Doone*, visits a memorial to the author, then heads to Oare. After following the Oare Water, it's a stiff climb back to County Gate.

View over Malmsmead and Lorna Doone Country from near County Gate

SHORT WALKS EXMOOR

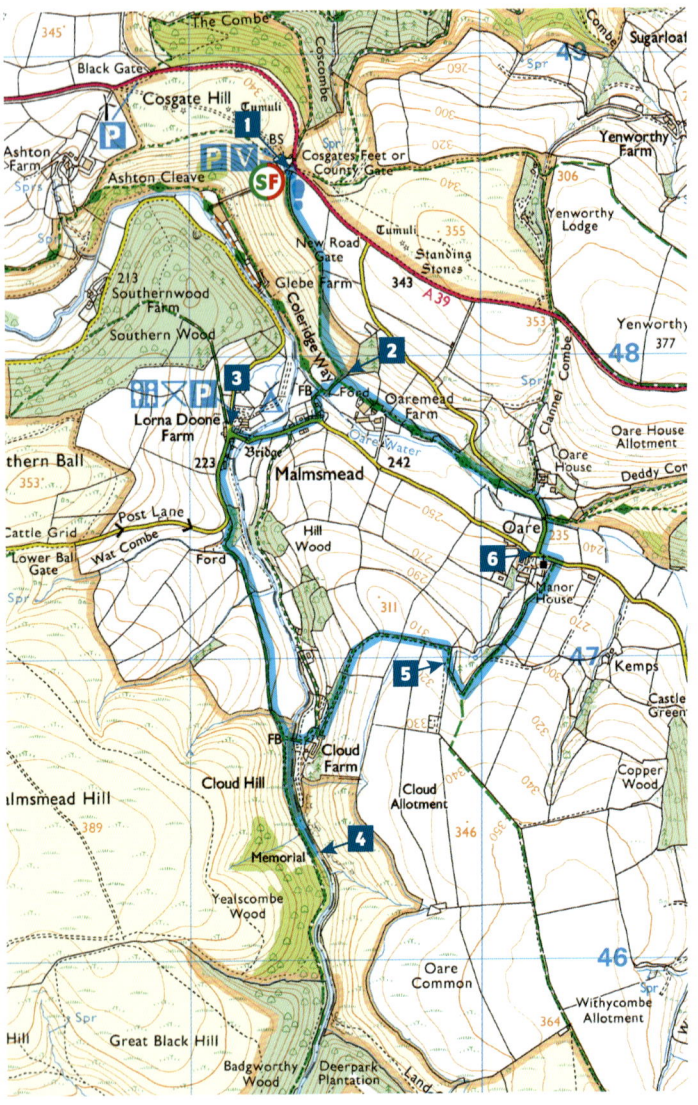

The bridge and ford across the Badgworthy Water at Malmsmead

1 At the car park entrance with the A39 ahead, turn right through a field gate. Follow the bridleway downhill towards Malmsmead, with a fence on the left, enjoying the view over the hills and valleys of Lorna Doone Country. Continue downhill to a three-way bridleway junction.

2 Keep ahead between hedges to the **Oare Water**. Turn right, then left across the footbridge. Follow the enclosed bridleway and then bear right up the track. Turn right along the lane towards Malmsmead and cross the bridge over the Badgworthy Water to a junction beside **Lorna Doone Farm**.

3 Turn left up the lane signed to Fellingscott, Slocombeslad and Tippacott. As the lane bends right, fork left through a gate. Follow the track as it curves left and go through a gate. Head up the enclosed track, go through another gate and then down towards the footbridge. The onward route goes over the footbridge, but before doing that, keep ahead along the track for 400m to a **memorial** commemorating R D Blackmore and some seats beside the Badgworthy Water. This makes a great picnic spot.

4 Turn around, retrace your steps and turn right across the footbridge over the Badgworthy Water. Keep

Cloud Farm

ahead through the campsite to a track junction. Turn left and then immediately bear right towards **Cloud Farm**, before turning left up a track signed 'footpath to Oare church'. Go through a gate, continue uphill and go through another gate. Follow the left-hand boundary through three fields separated by gates and leave the third field through a gate to join a track.

5 Follow the enclosed track, which soon swings left. Where the track curves right, fork left down the grassy bridleway and go through a gate. Follow the left-hand boundary down to a gate and turn left along the lane, past **Oare church** on the left to reach a junction.

Published in 1869, R D Blackmore's romantic novel *Lorna Doone* is set amongst these brooding hills and valleys. Many place names appear in the novel and St Mary's Church in Oare was the setting for the marriage of the main characters, John Ridd and Lorna Doone.

6 Turn right (signed to Lynmouth and Porlock), cross the Oare Water and follow the lane round to the left. Just after the drive for **Oare House** on the right, fork left through a gate. Follow the grassy bridleway and then continue through three fields separated by gates, keeping to the right of **Oaremead Farm**. Go through a gate to

WALK 7 – LORNA DOONE COUNTRY

arrive back at the signed junction passed earlier (Waypoint 2). Turn right and retrace the outward route back up to **County Gate**. If you started at Malmsmead turn left and continue the instructions from Waypoint 2.

− To shorten

Miss out the steep section from County Gate by starting the walk at Malmsmead (Waypoint 3) beside Lorna Doone Farm (parking nearby). This reduces the walk by 1.5km (30min).

+ To lengthen

At Waypoint 4 you can continue along the tree-shaded valley, following the bridleway beside the Badgworthy Water as far as you like – but remember you will have to retrace your steps to complete the walk.

St Mary's Church, Oare

Porlock Weir

WALK 8
Porlock Weir and Culbone church

Start/finish	*Porlock Weir*
Locate	*///lightens.streaking.cities*
Cafes/pubs	*Pub and cafe in Porlock Weir*
Transport	*Buses from Porlock and Minehead stop at Porlock Weir*
Parking	*Car park in Porlock Weir (TA24 8PB)*
Toilets	*At car park*

Time 3hr
Distance 8.5km (5¼ miles)
Climb 400m

From Porlock Weir the route soon follows the coast path up through woods to a secluded church before heading back along the Coleridge Way

From the harbour settlement of Porlock Weir with its picturesque thatched buildings, the route soon makes a steady climb (which is steep at first) through Yearnor Wood up to Culbone church. Then it's another steep climb up towards Silcombe Farm. From here the walk becomes easier, following the Coleridge Way along quiet lanes before heading down through Worthy Wood back to Porlock Weir.

St Beuno's Church, Culbone

1 Stand beside the coast path signpost, facing the 15th-century thatched Ship Inn with the car park and sea behind you. Cross the road and pass between the Ship Inn (left) and the Porlock Weir Hotel (right). Follow the path as it bends to the right and heads uphill. Go through a gate, continue alongside the right-hand field edge to another gate, then along the enclosed path. Keep left up the track to a lane. Turn right along the lane (a bridleway

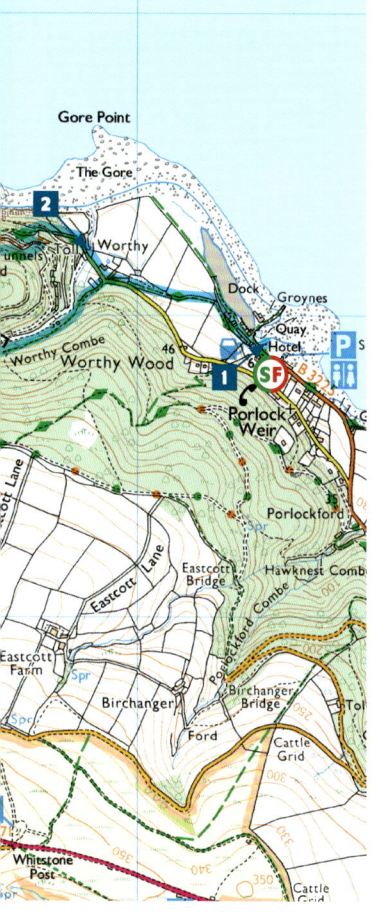

2 Later the coast path joins from the right. Follow this up through **Yearnor Wood**, passing through two short tunnels on the way; keep a lookout for the coast path signage at junctions. Later, follow a track as it curves right past a stone building on your left to a signed junction. Turn right and shortly turn right again to enter the churchyard at **Culbone**. St Beuno's Church, which dates from the Saxon and Norman periods, is claimed to be the smallest complete parish church in England.

3 After visiting the church, pass the large cross and head to the far-left corner of the churchyard. Go through the small gate and turn right, following a path up beside a stream. Pass under the track used earlier and then pass a house. Continue up through Withy Wood to a track and turn left. Go through a gate, keep ahead and go through another gate to join a lane near **Silcombe Farm**.

4 Turn left, now following the **Coleridge Way**. The walk follows quiet lanes for 2.5km, passing the pretty cottages at Parsonage Farm on the way. At a junction with **Yarner Farm** to the left, keep ahead along the lane signed 'Porlock Weir via the Worthy Toll Road'. The lane heads downhill to a junction. Turn sharp left for 200m and fork right along a track, signed to Porlockford and Porlock.

on the left is the return route) to the thatched **Worthy Toll House** with its two archways. Go through the right-hand arch, signed to Culbone church.

Cottage at Parsonage Farm

The Coleridge Way – waymarked with a quill pen symbol – explores the landscape that inspired the English poet Samuel Taylor Coleridge (1172–1834), who wrote *The Rime of the Ancient Mariner* and *Kubla Khan*.

5 Cross a stream at Yearnor Mill Bridge and at the Y-junction, fork left down the bridleway, signed to Worthy. Follow this down through **Worthy Wood**, keeping parallel with a stream on the left, to a junction at the bottom. Turn right along the lane used earlier and after 70m fork left along a track to retrace the outward route back to the start.

> **– To shorten**
>
> At Waypoint 3, after visiting Culbone church, retrace the outward route back to Porlock Weir. This reduces the walk by 2.5km (1hr).

Worthy Toll House

Tunnels and programming

The tunnels on the way to Culbone church were once part of the gardens at Ashley Combe House (now demolished). This was the home of William King who married Ada, daughter of the poet Lord Byron and Annabella Milbanke. It was here that Ada (a noted writer and mathematician) and Charles Babbage, professor of mathematics at Cambridge University, are said to have walked while discussing the mathematical principles behind his 'Difference Engine' or 'mechanical calculating machine'. Ada wrote a mathematical sequence that computer historians regard as the first computer program. The modern 'Ada' programming language is named in her honour.

Tarr Steps clapper bridge across the River Barle

WALK 9
Tarr Steps and the River Barle

Start/finish	*Tarr Steps car park*
Locate	*///forest.corrosive.spoiler (arrive from the Winsford Hill side)*
Cafes/pubs	*Pub/cafe at Tarr Farm*
Transport	*No public transport*
Parking	*Tarr Steps car park (TA22 9QA)*
Toilets	*At car park*

Time 1½hr
Distance 4.5km (2¾ miles)
Climb 180m

Cross a popular clapper bridge, wander along a wooded riverside path and return through open fields

After crossing the picturesque Tarr Steps clapper bridge this walk meanders through woodland beside the River Barle before crossing back via a footbridge. Then it's off up Watery Lane – as the name suggests it can be a bit wet after heavy rain – to Knaplock. From here head down through fields, admiring the views on the way back towards Tarr Steps. A slightly shorter, and much easier, return is also given. If the river is in flood, save this walk for another day.

The River Barle in autumn

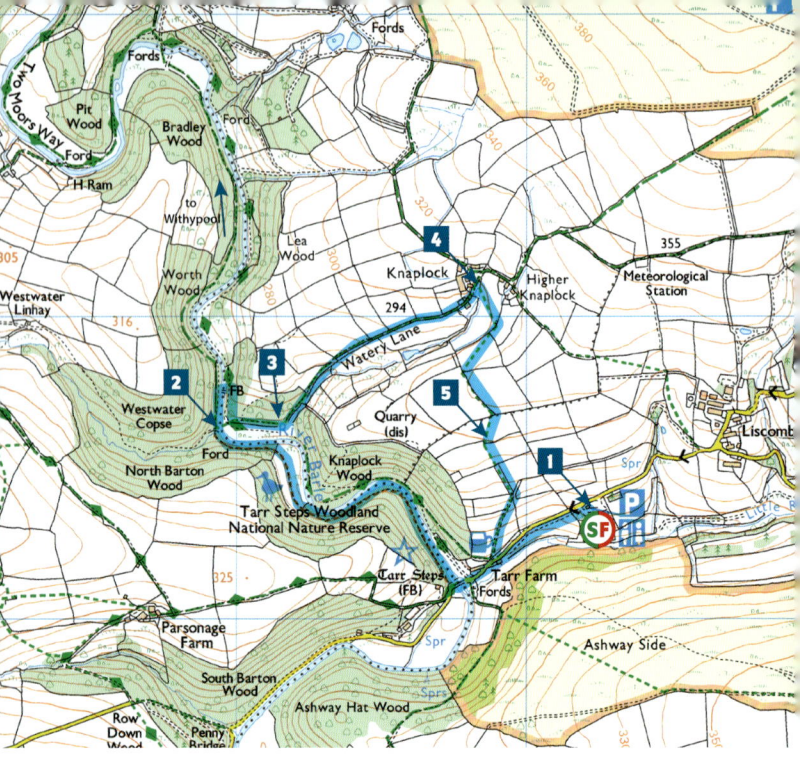

1 Leave the car park from near the exit and follow the path downhill, parallel with the lane on the other side of the hedge. Later, join the lane and continue down past Tarr Farm Inn (which dates from the 1600s) to the **River Barle**. With care, cross via the ancient **Tarr Steps** clapper bridge.

> The bridge was first mentioned in Tudor times. At 55m long, it is the longest bridge of its kind in Britain, and has 17 spans, with the flat covering stones lying on top of stone pillars. The name 'clapper' is probably from the Anglo-Saxon *cleaca* meaning stepping stone.

Once across the bridge turn right and follow the riverside path (circular walk), upstream through woodland. The woodland is a mix of oak, ash, beech and sycamore and is home to dormice and rare lichens. After just over 1km reach a small stone clapper bridge.

Tarr Steps

2 Cross the bridge over the stream (West Water) and continue for 130m to a junction beside a footbridge. To lengthen the walk continue upstream. Turn right across the footbridge over the River Barle to a junction and turn right for 300m, passing a flat grassy area – an ideal place for a picnic – to reach a junction with a stream and footbridge ahead.

3 Turn left up **Watery Lane** (signed 'bridleway Winsford Hill via Knaplock'). Alternatively, to shorten the walk keep straight ahead along the river. Go through a gate and up the stony, sunken track. Continue through two more gates, then pass a cottage (left) and barn (right) to a track junction on your left at **Knaplock Farm**. Turn right across the grass, step over the stream and go through the kissing gate.

4 Bear half-right across the field to the hedge. Go through a gate, turn right and go through another gate. Head up to the top right field corner, go through the kissing gate and turn

Views over fields near Knaplock

left along the field edge to the corner. Go through another kissing gate, head diagonally right across the field and through a field gate.

5 Bear slightly left downhill with views over the wooded valley ahead, passing through a gate on the way and leave through another gate. Follow the grassy track down to the bottom right field corner. Go through the gate and down the track to the lane beside Tarr Farm Inn. Turn left for a few paces and then pass through the hedge gap on the right and retrace your steps back up to the car park.

> **− To shorten**
> At Waypoint 3 keep ahead across the footbridge and follow the signed circular walk back to Tarr Steps and the car park. This saves 1km (30min).

> **+ To lengthen**
> At the footbridge that crosses the River Barle (between Waypoints 2 and 3) follow the signposted Two Moors Way upstream towards Withypool as far as you like – but remember you will have to retrace your steps to complete the walk.

WALK 10
Dunkery Beacon

Start/finish	*Dunkery Gate and Bridge*
Locate	*///stub.seatbelt.transcribes*
Cafes/pubs	*None on route*
Transport	*No public transport*
Parking	*Car park at Dunkery Bridge (TA24 7EE)*
Toilets	*No public toilets on route*

Choose a fine day for this walk up Dunkery Beacon – Exmoor's highest summit – from where there are far-reaching views. After a gradual ascent to the summit, the route heads downhill to explore the northern slope of Dunkery Beacon, following Dicky's Path and visiting wooded Sweetworthy Combe. Climb back up to the ridge to visit Great Rowbarrow before heading back to Dunkery Bridge. A shorter walk with less climbing is also possible.

Time 2¾hr
Distance 7.5km (4¾ miles)
Climb 305m

Choose a clear day for a walk up to Exmoor's highest summit to enjoy the views

Stone cairn on top of Dunkery Beacon

SHORT WALKS EXMOOR

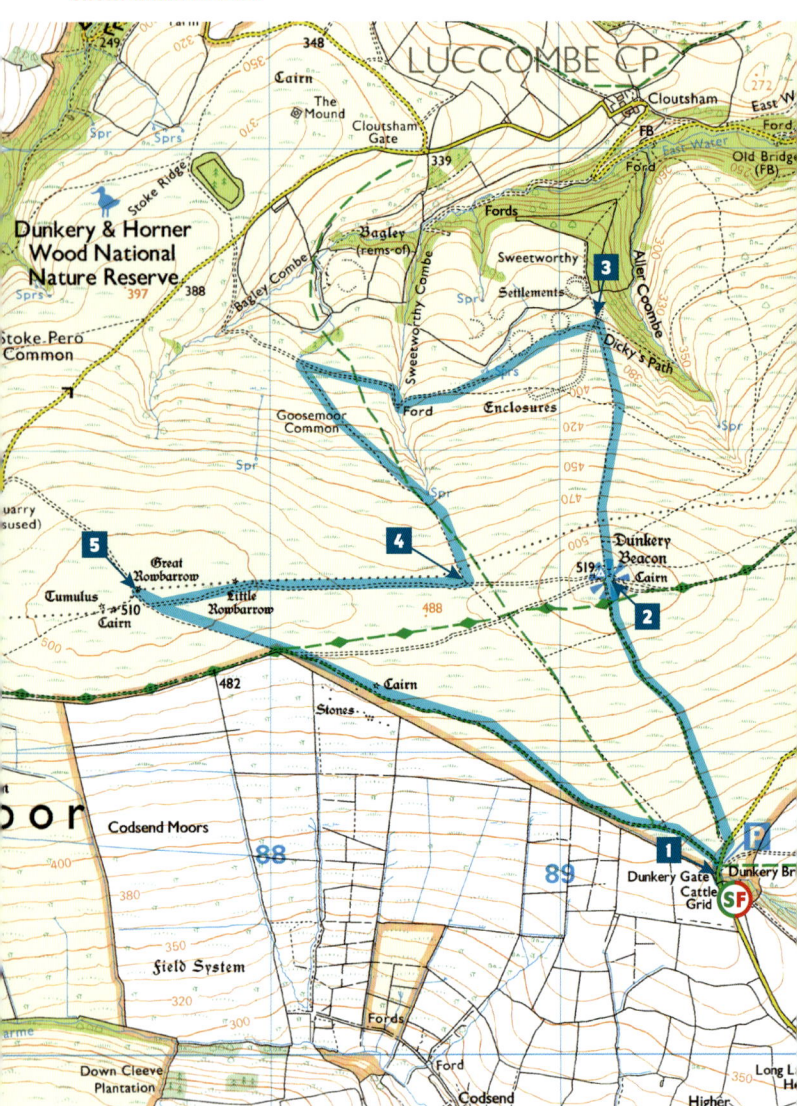

64

Heading down towards Dicky's Path

1 From Dunkery Bridge walk up the road for 100m (do not take the path opposite the car park – that is the return route) and turn left at the fingerpost, along the bridleway to Dunkery Beacon. Continue steadily uphill to the large stone cairn built on top of a Bronze Age burial mound on the summit of **Dunkery Beacon**.

2 To continue the main walk go straight on past the stone cairn, heading downhill towards the Bristol Channel. For a shorter walk take the first path on the left as you arrive at the stone cairn. After 100m keep ahead at a path junction, heading downhill to a junction with **Dicky's Path**, where you turn left. To visit Aller Coombe with its pretty little waterfall turn right for 250m, then retrace your steps.

3 Continue along the fairly level Dicky's Path. This area, known as Sweetworthy, contains the remains of two Iron Age enclosures or settlements. Soon there is a line of trees

Approaching the wooded Sweetworthy Combe

Heading over Dunkery Hill towards Little Rowbarrow

over to your right before you reach wooded **Sweetworthy Combe**. Cross the small stream (there is no footbridge so this might be difficult after heavy rain) and continue along the path for 300m to a junction on the left. Turn sharp left, following the path up to the broad ridge, and then turn right.

4 Follow the wide path up to a small stone cairn on the right, known as **Little Rowbarrow**. Continue for 300m to a junction where the track curves to the right. The walk turns sharp left here on a narrow path, but before that follow the track to the right for 50m to visit **Great Rowbarrow**.

5 Retrace your steps to the junction and fork right. Head gently downhill on the narrow path for 500m through the heather to a junction near a wall corner, then keep ahead, ignoring a track to the left (this is the shorter walk). Follow the stony track downhill, with the wall over to the right, back to the road at **Dunkery Bridge** opposite the car park.

The large circular mounds of stones that can be seen at Great Rowbarrow and Little Rowbarrow are the remains of two Bronze Age burial cairns; 100m to the west of Great Rowbarrow is a third burial cairn.

SHORT WALKS EXMOOR

Dunkery Beacon

The view over the Bristol Channel from Dunkery Beacon

Dunkery Beacon (519m) is both the highest point in Exmoor and Somerset and the highest point in Southern England outside of Dartmoor. Views from this lofty position on a clear day are extensive: north across the Bristol Channel to Wales and the Brecon Beacons; south-west to Dartmoor; and much nearer to north-east is Selworthy Beacon (Walk 12). A toposcope on the summit allows you to identify more places. The stone cairn and plaque, erected on top of a Bronze Age burial mound, commemorate the donation of Dunkery Hill to the National Trust in 1935.

— To shorten

On reaching Dunkery Beacon (Waypoint 2) take the first wide path on the left and follow it for 1km down to a T-junction, with trees and bushes ahead, and turn left down the track to Dunkery Bridge. This saves 3.5km (1hr 15min) and 175m of climbing.

WALK 11
Allerford and Selworthy

Start/finish	Allerford
Locate	///gasp.reading.violinist
Cafes/pubs	Tea room at Selworthy
Transport	Buses between Porlock and Minehead/Lynmouth stop on the A39 at Allerford (100m off route)
Parking	Car park in Allerford (TA24 8HN), or Selworthy
Toilets	Allerford and Selworthy

Time 2¾hr
Distance 8.5km (5¼ miles)
Climb 350m

A hilly walk with pretty villages and coastal views on part of the Holnicote Estate

Take a stroll through the picturesque neighbouring hamlets of Allerford and Selworthy, then head up Selworthy Combe to Selworthy Beacon. After soaking up the views from the top, head down along the broad ridge for a while before skirting round Bossington Hill. The final section takes you down through Allerford Plantation back to Allerford.

Thatched cottage at Selworthy Green

SHORT WALKS EXMOOR

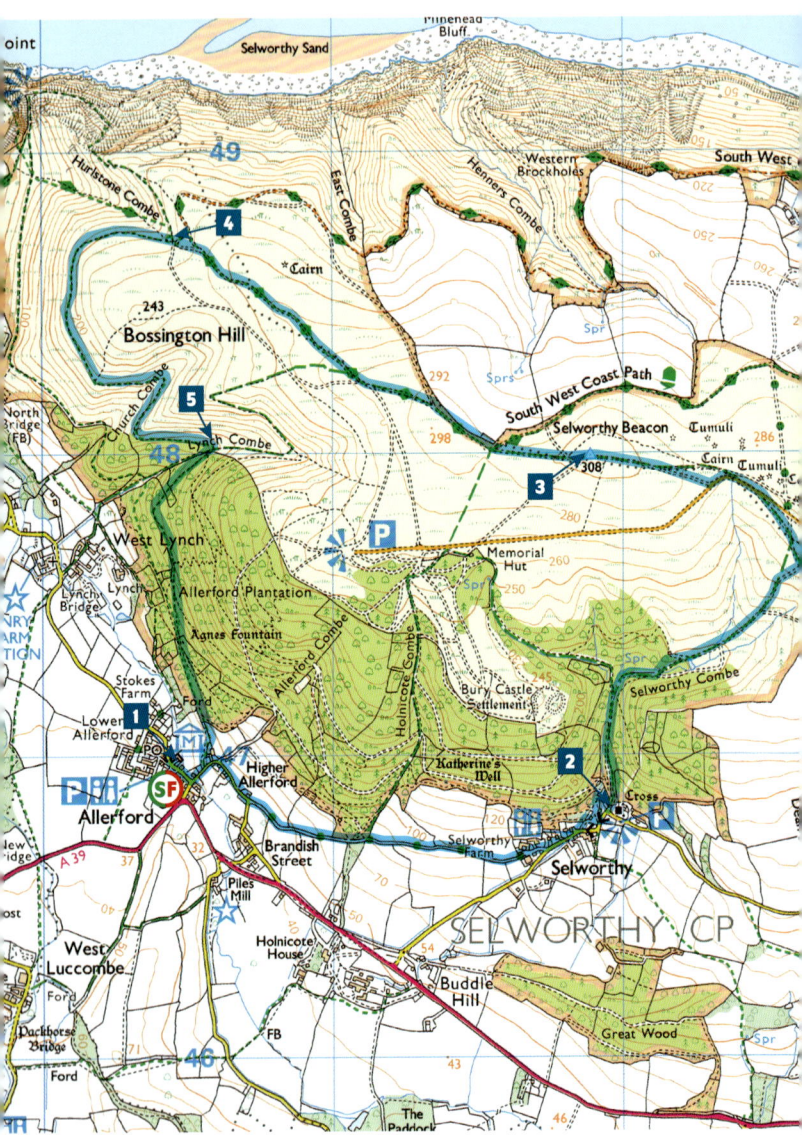

70

Picture-perfect Allerford with its bridge over the River Aller

1 Stand facing the Allerford Museum and turn right along the road. At the corner, turn left across the scenic footbridge over the River Aller and head up the lane. If you are starting from the bus stop on the A39, head to the junction, turn left along the lane and keep ahead across the footbridge. Follow the lane as it swings right and where it swings right again, fork left (straight on) along a hedge-lined track to a junction with a lane. Turn left through **Selworthy** and immediately after passing the toilets (left), turn left through a small gate. Follow the tarmac path through Selworthy Green with its pretty thatched cottages, continue up past the Periwinkle Tea Room and follow the tarmac path to the right. Go through the gate beside the war memorial to a signed junction. Ahead along the lane is the white-washed 14th-century All Saints Church.

2 Turn left along the track, go through a gate to a split and fork right (straight on) along a bridleway for 300m. At the four-way junction keep ahead with a stream on your left and follow the track as it curves to the right. At the next junction, fork left (signed to Selworthy Combe) across the stream. Keep ahead up **Selworthy Combe** to a cross-track junction near the top and turn left (signed to Selworthy Beacon). Bear left along the access road and, as it swings left, fork right up a track to the top of **Selworthy Beacon** with its cairn and trig point.

Selworthy Beacon

Selworthy Combe is one of six combes carved by streams on the sides of Bossington Hill. The word 'combe' comes from the Welsh word *cwm*, meaning valley.

3 From the trig point keep ahead (the wide path to the left is the shortcut). At a signed bridleway junction keep ahead along the main track (bridleway to Hurlstone) and 40m after a track joins from the left, fork right (footpath to Hurlstone) down the track. At the next split keep left downhill towards Bossington and then straight on at a crossing path for 25m to a signed four-way junction beside a seat on the right.

4 Keep left (footpath to Lynch Combe) and follow the narrow, fairly level path skirting anti-clockwise round **Bossington Hill**, enjoying the coastal views on the way. Follow the path as it loops round Church Combe and soon enters trees. The path swings left and then crosses a stream (there is no footbridge) in **Lynch Combe**.

5 Turn right, then immediately fork left through a small gate, now following signs for Allerford. Continue down the main path through **Allerford Plantation** to a six-way path junction beside St Agnes Fountain. Keep ahead down the right-hand fork. Go through two gates a few metres apart and continue down through the field, keeping to the left. Go through a gate to a lane and turn right down towards **Allerford**. Now retrace your steps back to the car park.

> **— To shorten**
>
> At Waypoint 3, fork half-left down to the access road, turn right for 150m, then left along a bridleway (signed to Allerford) and follow this down Holnicote Combe to join the track used earlier and turn right back to Allerford. This shortens the walk by 2km (30min).

WALK 11 – ALLERFORD AND SELWORTHY

Holnicote Estate

Sir Thomas Acland (7th Baronet) of Killerton acquired the Holnicote Estate in 1745 through his marriage to Elizabeth Dyke. The estate not only includes Allerford and Selworthy but also Dunkery Beacon (Walk 10). Holnicote passed down through the generations until Sir Richard Dyke Acland, 15th Baronet, donated both Holnicote and Killerton to the National Trust in 1944. The picture-postcard thatched cottages around Selworthy Green were built by Sir Thomas Dyke Acland in 1828 for estate pensioners; one now houses the Periwinkle Tea Room.

Following the path round Bossington Hill with a view over Porlock Bay

Statue of Lorna Doone near Exford House

WALK 12
Dulverton and Marsh Bridge

Start/finish	*Lorna Doone statue, Dulverton*
Locate	*///bandaged.farm.snipe*
Cafes/pubs	*Pubs and cafes in Dulverton, tea room at Marsh Bridge*
Transport	*Buses from Minehead, Taunton and Tiverton stop at the High Street (join the walk at the Bridge Inn)*
Parking	*Car park beside Exmoor House (TA22 9HL), or car park in the High Street*
Toilets	*On the High Street opposite the junction with Union Street*

Time 2hr
Distance 5.5km (3½ miles)
Climb 230m

Explore a historic market town and walk along riverside and woodland paths, including a short, steep climb

The historic market town of Dulverton is tucked in the south-east corner of Exmoor and often said to be the southern gateway to Exmoor. This route follows the River Barle upstream past Burridge Wood to Marsh Bridge. After you cross the river, there is a stiff climb up through Looseall Wood before a gentler meander leads back down to Dulverton.

The medieval bridge over the River Barle

1 From the car park turn left along the access road to reach the Lorna Doone statue on the small green. Over to the right is Exmoor House – originally the 19th-century Dulverton Union Workhouse – which now houses the Exmoor National Park Authority. Continue along the access road to the junction with the road (B3222) beside the Bridge Inn on your left. Turn right across the medieval bridge over the **River Barle** and immediately turn right along Oldberry Lane. At the sharp left-hand bend, fork right up the lane, keeping right to reach a Y-junction.

2 Fork right, following the Exe Valley Way along the edge of **Burridge Wood** (ignoring a path on the left). The wood

The old packhorse bridge near Marsh Bridge

is a mix of sessile oak, ash and beech, crowned by the earthworks of Iron Age Oldberry Castle. The track makes a sweeping loop with the river over to the right. Keep ahead along the track as it swings right (ignoring a path to the left), crossing a small stream (no footbridge) on the way. Go through a gate, pass some houses at **Kennel Farm** and go through another gate. Bear right along the minor road to **Marsh Bridge**, passing Marsh Bridge Cottage B&B and tea garden on the left.

3 Cross the bridge over the River Barle and immediately after turn right and cross the old stone packhorse bridge to rejoin the minor road at a junction. Cross straight over and follow the lane up to meet the B3223. Cross over and follow the track opposite (restricted byway to Court Down and Northcombe) steeply up through **Looseall Wood**. Keep straight ahead as a track joins from the right and reach a T-junction at the top, near a seat. To lengthen the walk turn left.

4 Turn right and follow the track, which is fairly level to start with before it descends to **Dulverton**. On reaching the Old School House on your right, bear left and then right down some steps to pass All Saints Church. Continue along Bank Square to a cross-junction. To the left is Union Street and then the High Street (toilets and alternative car park). Cross straight over and continue down Fore Street, passing the town hall on your left. Keep right along the High Street

77

(B3223), passing the bus stop and crossing a bridge over Mill Leat, then continue along Bridge Street (B3223). A plaque on the wall on your left shows the height of the River Barle during the 1952 Lynmouth Flood. Turn right just after the Bridge Inn back towards Exmoor House and the Lorna Doone statue.

> **− To shorten**
>
> For a more level (though not shorter) walk, on reaching Marsh Bridge (Waypoint 3) turn around and retrace your outward route back to the start.

> **+ To lengthen**
>
> At Waypoint 4, turn left along the track, go through the field gate and turn right up alongside the field boundary. Go through a small gate and keep ahead to the trig point on Court Down. Turn around and retrace your steps, with views ahead. Adds 1km (30min).

Dulverton

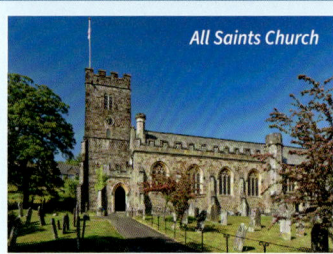

All Saints Church

Dulverton is a former mill town on the banks of the River Barle. The mills, first mentioned in the 14th century, were powered by water taken from the river at a large weir and diverted along a leat that still dissects the town. The 19th-century town hall in Fore Street, with its double external stairs and canopied porch, stood in as the dance hall in the 1988 film *The Land Girls*. All Saints Church, although extensively rebuilt by the Victorians, still has its 15th-century tower. Learn more about Dulverton at the Heritage Centre (follow the signed path on the right from beside the National Park Centre and library in Fore Street).

WALK 13
Haddon Hill and Wimbleball Lake

Time 2½hr
Distance 8km (5 miles)
Climb 175m

Enjoy views from Haddon Hill, explore the open heathland – good for seeing Exmoor ponies – and visit a dam

Start/finish	Haddon Hill car park
Locate	///amuse.populate.sailors
Cafes/pubs	None on route (cafe 4km off route at Wimbleball Lake)
Transport	No public transport
Parking	Haddon Hill car park, accessed from B3190 (TA4 2DS)
Toilets	At car park

The first part of this relatively easy walk follows tracks and paths as it heads over open heath, visiting Haddon Hill with its views over Wimbleball Lake before meandering alongside woodland. After a quick visit to the dam, it's off through a meadow before climbing up through woods. The final section follows a level route along the top edge of the heath back to the car park. The walk can easily be split into two shorter loops, if preferred.

Wimbleball Lake

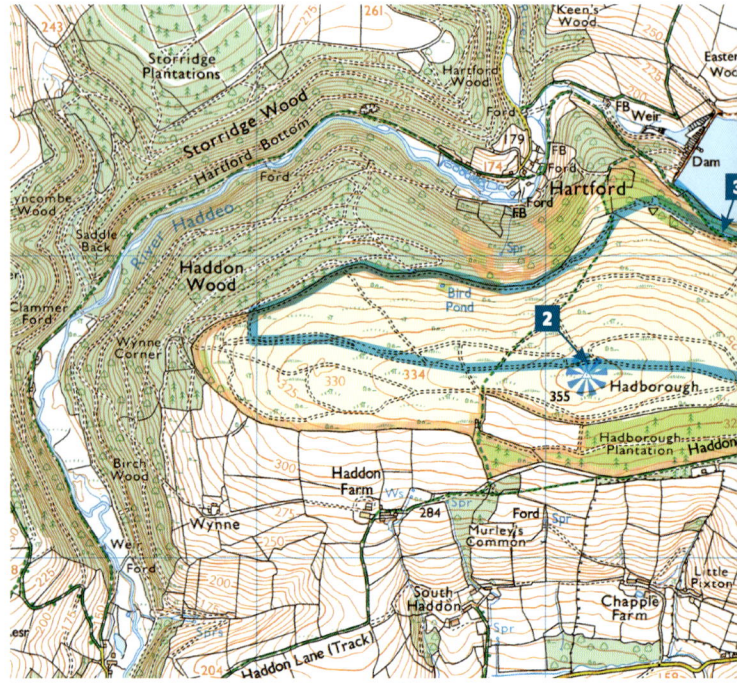

1 Head to the far-left corner of the car park and go through the gate to a three-way junction. Take the right-hand track and after 15m bear left. Keep ahead along the track up to the top of **Haddon Hill** – the trig point (355m) is over to the left of the track.

> The open moor of Haddon Hill is a great place to see Exmoor ponies, typically a rich brown colour, often with a pale muzzle and underbelly. Their teeth are adapted to allow them to graze coarse vegetation such as gorse and bramble.

2 Continue straight on along the main track, heading downhill for 1km, ignoring crossing routes. On reaching a T-junction, turn right down towards a gate with trees ahead. Do not go through the gate, but instead turn right and follow the track for just under 1.5km. Ignore a crossing path and follow the track as it curves right and

WALK 13 – HADDON HILL AND WIMBLEBALL LAKE

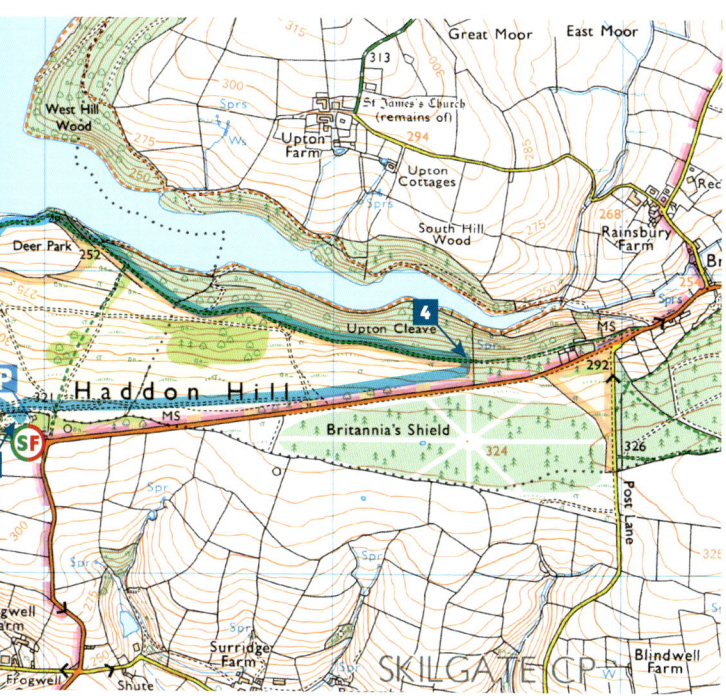

then keep right at a split junction to reach a tarmac access track.

3 The onward route is the track opposite, but before that turn left down the tarmac track to visit the reservoir **dam**. Retrace your steps to the junction and turn left. Alternatively, for a shorter walk turn right uphill. Follow the bridleway (signed to Upton) down through the trees. Go through a gate and follow the track through the open meadow, with views of **Wimbleball Lake** to your left.

> A man-made reservoir with a 49m-high dam, Wimbleball Lake can hold 21 billion litres of water. The lake and its surroundings are managed for wildlife and recreation, and there is a dark sky discovery hub for viewing the night sky.

Leave through another gate and continue to a signed junction, then keep ahead along the track (the path to the right leads directly up to the car park). At a split, keep right and follow the track gently uphill. Some 25m before a gate ahead, a stony path heads up to the right.

4 Take this path to the right and follow it as it curves right up to a path junction at the top and bear right again. Continue, with the trees and road beyond over to the left, for just under 1.5km. On the way, look to your right across the valley to see St James' Tower, all that remains of Upton's 14th-century church. Cross straight over the tarmac access track and keep ahead for 100m, then turn left and go through a gate back to the car park.

— To shorten

Loop 1: Complete the walk as far as Waypoint 3, then turn right up the tarmac access track. On nearing the trees turn right and then left to the car park. This saves 3.5km (1hr).

Loop 2: At the far-left corner of the car park, go through the gate and turn sharp right to reach the tarmac access track. Turn left down to Waypoint 3 then turn right to join the main walk. This saves 3.5km (1hr).

+ To lengthen

Cross the dam and bear right, keeping the lake on your right, following a permissive footpath signed to 'Wimbleball Hub' where there is a seasonal cafe, toilets and parking. Retrace your steps to the dam to continue the walk. This adds 4km (1hr).

Trig point on Haddon Hill

WALK 14
Luxborough and Withycombe Common

Start/finish	Village hall, Luxborough
Locate	///reforming.boardroom.trio
Cafes/pubs	Pub at Luxborough (Kingsbridge)
Transport	No public transport
Parking	Beside the village hall (TA23 0SH)
Toilets	No public toilets on route

Time 2¾hr
Distance 9km (5½ miles)
Climb 310m

Explore a peaceful village hidden in the Brendon Hills and climb to a trig point with a view

Head to the Brendon Hills on the eastern side of Exmoor for a walk through the three hamlets that make up Luxborough. From Kingsbridge, home to the Royal Oak Inn, the walk goes up through Monkham Wood to the trig point on Withycombe Common. After admiring the views, head down tracks to arrive at Churchtown and St Mary's Church. The final section follows the valley, passing through Pooltown on the way back to the start. The walk can easily be shortened by missing out Withycombe Common.

Thatched cottage in Kingsbridge

SHORT WALKS EXMOOR

View of the Quantocks from Monkham Hill

1 With your back to the village hall in **Kingsbridge**, turn left along the lane to a junction and keep ahead towards Roadwater and Washford. To the left is the Royal Oak Inn. At the next junction, fork left (signed to Rodhuish and Withycombe), up past a house to a junction. Turn left and follow the track (bridleway) up through **Monkham Wood** to a junction at the top.

2 Turn right to continue with the main walk. Alternatively, for the shorter walk turn sharp left. Keep left at two track junctions to arrive at a four-way junction with a gate ahead and a lovely view of the Quantock Hills. Do not go through the gate, but instead turn left and follow the bridleway (signed to Dunster) alongside a fence on your right (this may be overgrown in summer). Go through a bridle gate and keep ahead to a junction with a track.

3 Bear left up the track (signed to Luxborough) to reach the trig point on **Withycombe Common**.

> The trig point (381m) is sited on a tumulus, or Bronze Age burial mound. From here there is a good view north across the Bristol Channel to Wales, and on clear days you can see the Brecon Beacons.

Continue down the track and go through a gate to arrive at the junction passed earlier (Waypoint 2). Cross over diagonally right and continue along the track opposite (signed as bridleway to Luxborough).

4 Keep left (straight on) at a track junction, heading downhill. A gate on the left along the way gives a good view – the farmland is private though. At a three-way track junction, keep left

Views on the way down to Churchtown

St Mary's Church in Churchtown

for a few paces, then turn left and immediately turn right. Continue downhill, through a gate and down between hedges. Go through gates either side of a field, then down past a cottage to a minor road in **Churchtown**.

5 Turn left, and as the road swings right, fork left past a house to visit St Mary's Church. Return to the road and turn left to a junction. Fork right downhill, following the lane as it crosses a bridge and then swings left to a track junction on the left.

6 Fork left down the track (signed to Luxborough), then continue along the path to another track. Turn left down this past a cottage. Continue along the path through **Church Wood**, following the path as it curves right to reach a lane at **Pooltown**. Turn left, crossing the bridge over the Washford River and follow the lane back to the village hall and car park on your left.

SHORT WALKS EXMOOR

− To shorten

At Waypoint 2 turn sharp left and follow the track to a junction and continue the directions from Waypoint 4. This shortens the walk by 3km (45min).

> ⓘ *Nutcombe Bottom on the north side of Croydon Hill is home to the Tall Trees Trail, a short, easy access trail passing some of England's tallest trees, including a Douglas fir standing at just over 60m.*

Luxborough

Luxborough consists of three hamlets – Kingsbridge, Pooltown and Churchtown. St Mary's Church in Churchtown has a distinctive saddleback-roofed tower, and parts of the building date from the 13th century. Inside is a colourful Millennium stained-glass window by a local craftsman. Pooltown is named after the large pools along the Washford River. Kingsbridge has thatched cottages and the Royal Oak Inn, parts of which date from the 14th century.

Millennium stained-glass window in St Mary's Church

WALK 15
Dunster and Bat's Castle

Start/finish	National Park Centre, Dunster Steep
Locate	///profiled.midfield.rezoning
Cafes/pubs	Pubs and cafes in Dunster
Transport	Buses from Dulverton and Minehead stop along Dunster High Street
Parking	Dunster Steep car park (TA24 6SE)
Toilets	At car park

Time 2¼hr
Distance 7km (4½ miles)
Climb 240m

A historic village, an impressive castle, prehistoric settlements, woods and views

Historic and popular Dunster has a number of interesting sights, including the Yarn Market and the Priory Church of St George. The impressive castle and its subtropical gardens are well worth a visit. Leaving the village by the medieval Gallox Bridge, the walk makes a steady and lengthy climb on tracks up through woodland to Gallox Hill. After passing over Bat's Castle, it's then downhill all the way on tracks and paths, later heading through a former deer park, with a view of Dunster Castle.

Dunster Castle viewed from Dunster Park

SHORT WALKS EXMOOR

1 Exit the car park and turn left along Dunster Steep (A396) to the National Park Centre on the left. Continue along Dunster Steep and keep left along the High Street, passing the Luttrell Arms (left) and the Yarn Market (right). The octagonal, 17th-century timber-framed Yarn Market harks back to Dunster's once-flourishing cloth trade. At the traffic lights (just

WALK 15 – DUNSTER AND BAT'S CASTLE

after passing the bus stop), where the main road swings right, fork left (straight on) up Castle Hill and shortly afterwards keep right with the castle entrance to your left. Follow the lane down to West Street (A396).

2 Turn left along the pavement for 120m, then left along Mill Lane, soon with the mill leat on your left, to reach a junction. Ahead is the Water Mill Tea Room and Victorian watermill (National Trust). There has been a watermill on this site since the Domesday Book. Turn right along the tarmac bridleway (signed to Gallox Bridge), then turn left along Park Street past thatched cottages to the River Avill. Cross **Gallox Bridge** – a medieval packhorse bridge – and keep ahead along the track past a thatched cottage on the right to a three-way split junction.

3 Keep ahead (bridleway to Bat's Castle), following the tree-shaded track uphill (the left-hand option will be your return route). Keep right along the bridleway at a split and at the next split, fork left up a track (signed as

The Yarn Market, Dunster

Thatched cottage in Dunster

WALK 15 – DUNSTER AND BAT'S CASTLE

footpath to Bonniton Gate). At the left-hand bend, some 200m to the right is a viewpoint at Black Ball. At the next track junction, turn sharp left uphill. Turn right through a gate and continue up **Gallox Hill**, passing to the left of Black Ball Camp earthworks.

4 Head down to a slight dip, then keep ahead up to **Bat's Castle**. The earthworks of Bat's Castle, like Black Ball Camp, date from the Iron Age. Pass through the earthworks and keep ahead down to a junction with Withycombe Hill Gate ahead. Go through the gate and turn left down **Park Lane** (restricted byway). At the sharp right bend, turn left and go through **Carhampton Gate**.

5 Continue through **Dunster Park** (a former deer park), soon with a view of Dunster Castle and Conygar Tower, a folly. Later bear left and keep ahead through a gate to a junction (Waypoint 3). Turn right and retrace the route across Gallox Bridge and back to the main road (A396). Turn right for 120m.

6 As the church comes into view, turn left across the road and follow St George's Street to a junction. Turn right along Priory Green, with the Priory Church of St George on your right. Originally built by William de Mohun in

A seat beside Bat's Castle with a view over wooded Wootton Common

the 11th century, the present church dates mainly from the 15th century. Pass the late medieval dovecote (left) and then the tithe barn (right). Follow the road as it curves right and becomes The Ball, to reach a junction with the A396. Carefully cross over and turn left along Dunster Steep back to the National Park Centre and the car park.

> ⓘ *Head over to Dunster station and hop on the West Somerset Railway. The line, which operates between Minehead and Bishops Lydeard, is the longest standard-gauge independent heritage railway in the UK (www.west-somerset-railway.co.uk).*

— To shorten

For a much shorter walk, on reaching Gallox Bridge turn around, retrace your steps to West Street and turn right for 120m. Follow the walk instructions from Waypoint 6 past the church and back to the start. This walk is an easy 2km (40min).

Dunster Castle

View over Dunster Park to Dunster Castle

Dunster, or 'Dunn's Torre', was given to the de Mohun family soon after William the Conqueror became King of England. The castle was purchased by the Luttrell family in 1375 and it stayed in the family for 600 years until it was gifted to the National Trust in 1976. In the late 19th century George Luttrell was responsible for having the castle converted to the present, rather grand, Victorian country home. As well as the house and subtropical gardens there is a historic working watermill passed on the walk (www.nationaltrust.org.uk).

USEFUL INFORMATION

Tourism bodies

Exmoor National Park www.exmoor-nationalpark.gov.uk

Visit Exmoor www.visit-exmoor.co.uk

Tourist information

National Park centres

Dulverton, tel 01398 323841

Dunster, tel 01643 821835

Lynmouth, tel 01598 752509

Visitor information centres

Combe Martin, tel 01271 883319

Minehead, tel 01643 702624

Porlock, tel 01643 863150

Watchet, tel 01984 632101

Travel

Train enquiries

National Rail

tel 08457 484950

www.nationalrail.co.uk

Bus timetables

Traveline

tel 0871 2002233

www.traveline.info

© Steve Davison 2024
First edition 2024
ISBN: 978 1 78631 190 0
eISBN: 978 1 78765 154 8

Printed in Czechia on behalf of Latitude Press Ltd on responsibly sourced paper.
A catalogue record for this book is available from the British Library.

© Crown copyright and database rights 2024 OS AC0000810376
All photographs are by the author unless otherwise stated.

CICERONE

Cicerone Press, Juniper House, Murley Moss, Oxenholme Road,
Kendal, Cumbria, LA9 7RL

www.cicerone.co.uk

Updates to this Guide

While every effort is made to ensure the accuracy of guidebooks as they go to print, changes can occur during the lifetime of an edition. Any updates that we know of for this guide will be on the Cicerone website (www.cicerone.co.uk/1190/updates), so please check before planning your trip. We also advise that you check information about transport, accommodation and shops locally. We are always grateful for updates, sent by email to updates@cicerone.co.uk.

Register your book: To sign up to receive free updates, special offers and GPX files where available, create a Cicerone account and register your purchase via the 'My Account' tab at www.cicerone.co.uk.